COMMENDATIONS

… I haven't seen anything like it for *helpful niche in the market … If, like* *pay the social cost of conditioning yc* *ᵤₑ ᵤy compulsive* *'humming', you should still buy this little volume for the serious advice it contains.*

> **Jonathan Stephen**
> **Principal, Wales Evangelical School of Theology and Director, Affinity**

Here is a relevant book in a day when preaching is beginning to make a comeback again after several arid decades. In much of our modern preaching, some good attention is being given to content and the integrity required for biblical ministry, but a great deal of catching up is necessary in terms of actual effective delivery. This book by an open-air preacher will help us in our public speaking—even if our voices never have quite the resonance of a John Chrysostom, a Whitefield or a Billy Graham. I certainly intend to put into prayerful practice the invaluable suggestions and exercises given us by Mike Mellor.

> **Rico Tice**
> **Co-author of** Christianity Explored **and Associate Minister at All Souls Church, London**

ACKNOWLEDGEMENTS

I would like to offer my sincere thanks to Lulu Housman, Voice Specialist in the Speech and Language Therapy department at West Middlesex University Hospital, not only for her extremely helpful Appendix on exercises, but also for her 'eagle eye' on all things medical that I have written concerning the voice.

My grateful thanks to Martyn Leggett, Associate Specialist in Ear, Nose and Throat surgery at Poole Hospital NHS Trust, for kindly providing a physiology of the voice, and to Kinga Scales, for the very helpful drawings.

I would also like to express my gratitude to Penny Cox, Speech and Language Therapist at Poole Hospital NHS Trust, for her help in getting my own voice back on track and for inspiring me to 'do something' in order to prevent my fellow preachers from travelling the 'silent road'!

Finally, I am indebted to my dear long-suffering wife, Gwen, who has had to endure my voice 'for better, for worse' for forty years.

MINISTERING
THE MASTER'S WAY

Look after your voice:

Taking care of the preacher's greatest asset

Mike Mellor

DayOne

©Day One Publications 2008
First printed 2008

A CIP record is held at the British Library

ISBN 978-1-84625-125-2

Published by Day One Publications, Ryelands Road, Leominster, HR6 8NZ
☎ 01568 613 740
FAX 01568 611 473
email—sales@dayone.co.uk
web site—www.dayone.co.uk
North American e-mail—usasales@dayone.co.uk

Cover designed by Wayne McMaster and printed by Gutenberg Press, Malta

CONTENTS

INTRODUCTION **7**

1 OUR 'TOOL OF THE TRADE' **8**

2 UNDERSTANDING THE VOICE **14**

3 IMPROVING OUR VOICES **22**

4 PRESERVING OUR VOICES **32**

APPENDIX 1 EXERCISES: BREATHING, PHYSICAL
FLEXIBILITY, WARMING UP, ARTICULATION **44**

APPENDIX 2 A PHYSIOLOGY OF VOICE **54**

APPENDIX 3 'ON THE VOICE' BY C. H. SPURGEON
(FROM LECTURES TO MY STUDENTS) **58**

FOR FURTHER HELP AND INFORMATION **84**

ENDNOTES **85**

INTRODUCTION

'Behold, I send my messenger ... The voice ...' (Mark 1:2–3, KJV).

Can there be a more pitiful sight in all nature than that of a God-sent preacher who is forced to be silent? We are not thinking here, however, of a silence brought about by pressure from ungodly sources, but that which has been enforced because of the preacher's own negligence concerning his voice.

During my own self-induced silence, I was shocked to discover just how many other preachers and pastors had been in the same position. It is out of deep conviction and with love for my fellow heralds of the Word, therefore, that this little book is written, and with the prayer that it may prevent many others from being robbed of hours, if not years, of vital ministry.

I may fail on various fronts. Some may find it too much of a 'How to ...' book, while others may be disappointed that I have not included more practical help and exercises. A further complaint could be that it is far too short to be of any real benefit. My goal, however, is not to produce another speech book (of which a good number can be found, usually aimed at actors or singers), but that the sense of our high calling as God's spokesmen may be rekindled and, as a consequence, our desire to care for the frail vehicle God has designed to convey his Word may be increased.

Our 'tool of the trade'

IN THIS CHAPTER

Care of your voice not unspiritual →

Uniqueness of your voice →

Being aware of how you sound →

Chapter 1

The things that count cannot be counted.

–Anon

As the hammer is to the carpenter, the scalpel to the surgeon, the trowel to the brick mason or the needle to the tailor, so the voice is to the preacher. Man's voice is the primary means God uses to deliver his Word to mankind, yet how often we who are called to impart the most important truths in the world are apt to neglect, if not wilfully abuse, our all-vital 'tool of the trade'!

Time given to the study of theology, exegesis, sermon structure, delivery and other important ingredients that serve to make a man a preacher of the Word is, we would all agree, time well spent, and to neglect these things would be deemed irresponsible. Yet for some reason, the preacher's voice—without which no sermon will reach the hearer's ear, no matter how brilliant a sermon it is—is often given no attention at all. Perhaps it's because we think it an unspiritual thing to consider the 'mechanics' of preaching in this way.

A. W. Tozer was a man highly respected among preachers in the last century and who was often called the 'twentieth-century prophet' because of his penetrating insight into the ailments of the modern church. Yet he was a preacher who realized only too well the need to give time and attention to his voice, as his biographer recalls:

> Tozer's speaking voice was not particularly strong, and there was a distinct nasal quality about it. He soon decided he needed to do something about this deficit. Typical of Tozer, he went to a bookstore and purchased a volume on voice training to learn all he could about voice control. In his office was a large copy of Milton's *Paradise Lost*. Tozer would place it on a music stand purchased from the sanctuary and read it aloud. He

read through the book at least four times in order to strengthen his voice and gain better control of it.

To strengthen his lungs, Tozer would blow up balloons. In his briefcase he carried a supply of balloons for this purpose. Vanity? No. Simply an effort to be his best in God's service.[1]

Unique gift

John the Baptist was, significantly, called the 'voice' (Mark 1:2–3) and was used in his day to impact a generation for God and prepare them to meet their Messiah. We should not minimize the emphasis God places upon human instrumentality and, in particular, the human voice. Your voice, just like your thumbprint or DNA, is a unique gift. Whether you like the sound of it or not (and most preachers claim not to), this voice is yours and it sets you apart from any other person. Some seem to have a natural preaching voice that booms like thunder and carries well, while others of us have a weak, 'small' voice that frustrates us because of the lack of power and penetration.

It is interesting to note how, in both Scripture and church history, God placed the right man in the right situation—despite the doubts his servants may have had! No doubt it was for this reason that Jeremiah was informed that his future ministerial gifts were formed in his mother's womb:

> The word of the LORD came to me, saying,
>   'Before I formed you in the womb I knew you,
>   before you were born I set you apart;
>   I appointed you as a prophet to the nations.'
> 'Ah, Sovereign LORD,' I said, 'I do not know how to speak; I am only a child.'
> But the LORD said to me, 'Do not say, "I am only a child." You must go to everyone I send you to and say whatever I command you.'
>
> (Jer. 1:4–7)

Despite a strong inner conviction that he was to be God's man for the hour, Moses also was slow to be convinced of this fact and not only doubted but even challenged God's wisdom:

> Moses said to the LORD, 'O Lord, I have never been eloquent, neither in the past nor since you have spoken to your servant. I am slow of speech and tongue.'
> The LORD said to him, 'Who gave man his mouth? Who makes him deaf or mute? Who gives him sight or makes him blind? Is it not I, the LORD? Now go; I will help you speak and will teach you what to say.'
>
> (Exod. 4:10–12)

A recognition and conviction of the sovereignty of God in the distribution of his gifts is of utmost importance. Yet, strangely, even those with high views of God's sovereignty often stumble here—perhaps because of seeking to cultivate a humble spirit. However, it is quite easy for a godly man to wander from the safe ground of humility and find himself trespassing on the forbidden territory of unbelief—and never without consequences!

> But Moses said, 'O Lord, please send someone else to do it.'
> Then the LORD's anger burned against Moses and he said, 'What about your brother, Aaron the Levite? I know he can speak well ...'
>
> (Exod. 4:13–14)

What a tragedy! How serious it is when our reluctance causes God to bypass us and look to someone else simply because of our mock humility, self-pity or unbelief!

Horses for courses

When God calls us to be his spokesmen, he knows well our frailties and is more than able to cope with them! We may be concerned about a lisp, a stammer or what we perceive to be a pathetic-sounding voice, but God has a sphere of service for us, and these things will not matter where he places us. But of course, if there are ways in which we can improve—and there always are—then naturally we are responsible for that. Hence this book.

It has been said that the preacher's job is to 'comfort the disturbed and disturb the comfortable'. There are times when our voices must bring healing, and other times, awakening; so it is no wonder that we look with holy envy at a brother whose voice seems perfect to produce the effect we are seeking to achieve. But we need to remember that God needs both a tender Richard Sibbes, the Puritan known as 'the Heavenly Doctor', and a John Knox, the Reformer who 'raised his voice like a trumpet' (Isa. 58:1) and awakened Scotland.

Sound matters

God has chosen to communicate through words, and those words are spoken through a man's voice. As we shall see later, there is a difference between voice and speech. How we sound is of the utmost importance; it's not just *what* we say, but also *how* we say it.

We can only imagine how Christ sounded when he commanded Lazarus to 'Come out!' from the tomb (John 11:43), or when, in that tension-filled room, the Lord of life spoke to a dead child these words: '*Talitha koum* (… Little girl, I say to you, get up!)' (Mark 5:41). And in what tone did he speak those great words of invitation: 'Come to me, all you who are weary and burdened, and I will give you rest' (Matt. 11:28)?

We are seeking to be powerful preachers, yet often we fail to recognize the importance of how we sound.

We read of a man like Joseph Alleine who, we are told, was '… infinitely and insatiably greedy for the conversion of souls and to this end he poured out his very heart in prayer and in preaching'. Such were his appeals while preaching that '… they quite overcame his hearers; he melted them and sometimes dissolved the hardest hearts'.[2]

Reading Alleine's *Alarm to the Unconverted*, you might be excused for thinking that he was a mere tub-thumping, hellfire preacher. The same might be said of George Whitefield or John Wesley. But such was the love and pathos found in these men's voices that hearts were melted and stubborn wills were brought into willing captivity to Jesus Christ. The Holy Spirit is pleased to use the voice of the man sent with the message.

God has given us voices that are capable of communicating a wide range of sounds and emotions. Some of us may lament the fact that we lack that big, commanding voice that others seem to own—certainly, a preacher must be heard. The good news is that we are not 'stuck' with a voice that cannot be improved and made powerful under the hand of God! Just as Tozer saw that it was his responsibility to 'do something', so we also need to grasp that it is dishonouring to God if we neglect to put in time and effort to improve this grand vehicle of communication with which he has provided us.

If modern-day sports stars were out of action or playing below par because of lack of care and exercise, it would be considered most unprofessional; yet large numbers of preachers experience voice problems out of failure to observe even the most basic rules of voice care. Singers, actors and schoolteachers seem to be more conscientious in this area than heralds of the gospel. This should never be so.

Hopefully, we are now convinced that our voices matter, and that we are responsible for their condition. In the coming chapters, therefore, we will look at understanding, improving and preserving this vital tool of the preacher's trade.

Understanding the voice

IN THIS CHAPTER

How the voice works →

The difference between voice and speech →

Voice qualities →

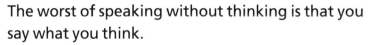

Chapter 2

The worst of speaking without thinking is that you say what you think.

–James Denney

We would all agree that to speak without giving thought to the content of our message would be the height of foolishness. Yet, in the context of caring for our God-given instrument for conveying God's Word, we need a realization that thought also needs to be given constantly to how we *deliver* the message.

In this chapter, we will be looking at understanding the voice, that is, how the voice works, the difference between voice and speech, and the tone we produce when we speak.

Begins in the mind

There is a process involved in producing the words we speak and, as with many other processes, it all begins in the mind:

- The brain sends signals to the body to prepare the breath for making the necessary sound.
- The breath travels up through the windpipe to the vocal cords (or vocal folds). These are fleshy curtain-like folds that open and close as we speak.
- The vocal cords vibrate and are amplified by various cavities—the chest, the pharynx, the nose and sinuses, and finally the mouth.
- It is then the work of the tongue and lips to convert these sounds into speech that will be recognized by our hearers.

The vocal cords

It is helpful to think of your voice as a musical instrument. The vocal cords can be seen as the strings of a violin, designed to produce sound. The stream of breath is like the bow, which, when drawn across the strings, produces sounds which resonate. While the violin body is used to throw that sound out, our bodies have built-in amplifiers, or *cavities*. (Warning: much harm can be done to the voice if speaking regularly at a raised volume with insufficient breath flow and failing to use the diaphragm correctly.)

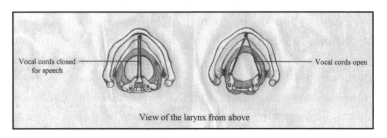

Vocal cords closed for speech

Vocal cords open

View of the larynx from above

Voice and speech

So, what is the difference between *voice* and *speech*?

Voice is the basic 'noise' produced when the breath 'plays' the vocal cords in the throat; *speech* is the process of converting that sound into actual words.

We are convinced that the preacher, above all public speakers, must be understood, so there is no point in his spending hours in preparation if the delivery is a mere jumble of noises. The apostle Paul, writing to the church in Corinth, warned, 'Unless you speak intelligible words with your tongue, how will anyone know what you are saying? You will just be speaking into the air' (1 Cor. 14:9).

C. H. Spurgeon, when lecturing his students, warned of 'that ghostly speech in which a man talks without using his lips, ventriloquizing most horribly'. Then he advised, '... open your mouths when you speak, for much inarticulate mumbling is the result of keeping the mouth half closed. It is not in vain that the New Testament evangelists have written of our Lord, "He opened his mouth and taught them."'[3]

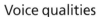

Voice qualities

PITCH

The voice can sound high or low. You must find that certain pitch at which your voice operates most comfortably without any straining.

Richard Bewes relates how Billy Graham, while being driven by car to a stadium to speak at a mission, would boom out, 'Yes, Yes, Yes, Yes!'[4] It may well have caused his passengers some discomfort, but this seasoned preacher no doubt was seeking to prepare his voice for the task ahead.

Of course, this does not mean that the voice should remain at that same pitch. What can be worse than having to listen to a voice that either drones on monotonously (unless invited to speak at the Annual Meeting of Insomniacs), or else yells endlessly at the same level?

John Wesley strongly warned his Methodist preachers of the latter danger, saying, 'For God's sake, don't scream.' Without doubt, harm will be done to preacher and hearer alike if this yelling continues.

The rule is: Don't force yourself to speak with either too high or too low a voice for a prolonged period.

VOLUME

The voice can speak loudly or softly. It is essential that the volume also varies throughout the message. The volume is adjusted by varying the pressure of the breath as it 'plays' the vocal cords. Attention given to breathing is vital. Much harm is caused by poor, shallow breathing, so we shall look later at exercises that will help us in this area. Singers especially realize only too well the importance of correct breathing and spend much time and effort working at this.

TONE

The message we have to convey is most vital but, as stated earlier, it is not only *what* we say but also *how* we say it that will affect our hearers. How does your voice sound? Nasal? Plummy? Raspy? Metallic and strident? We may give our hearers throbbing heads when we intended to give them throbbing hearts.

It is here that our inbuilt amplifiers, or *cavities*, play a major part and, when properly used, enable us to make the voice sound attractive to the ear—as well as save the larynx from major problems! (We will look at this in more on detail in Chapter 3.)

An awareness of the wide variety of tones of which your voice is capable is important. In his book *Physicians of Souls*, Dr Peter Masters lists some of them:

- a didactic voice
- an appealing voice
- an appreciative voice
- a surprised voice
- a warning voice
- a questioning voice
- an excited voice
- a sympathetic voice
- an amused voice
- a shocked voice
- a challenging voice
- a puzzled voice
- a pained voice.[5]

CLARITY

The voice is able to carry with less volume simply because of the clarity of our speech.

Some of us are mumblers, while many others simply speak far too quickly. This can, of course, be due to nerves.

Spurgeon remarks, 'Distinct utterance is far more important than wind power. Do give a word a fair chance, do not break its back in your vehemence, or run it off its legs in your haste.'[6]

Silence

There is 'a time to be silent and a time to speak' (Eccles. 3:7), and this is certainly true for the preacher. We must be aware of the danger of being 'speaking machines', simply churning out word after word without end, which only succeeds in tiring the listeners, causing them to switch off altogether.

No matter how interesting and attractive a voice may sound, silence really is golden at times, and it would be good for us to remember what is often called 'the power of the pause' and trust that it will be of benefit both to hearer and to preacher!

The wages of vocal abuse is …

It's not just preachers but also singers, schoolteachers, actors, aerobics teachers and enthusiastic soccer supporters who all run the risk of doing themselves harm through vocal abuse.

A few of the major problems are *polyps* (growths on the vocal cords), *nodules* (blister-like swellings just below the surface of the vocal cord) and *contact ulcers* (raw sores on the mucous membrane of the vocal cord). We will look at the possible damage done to the voice through neglect in more detail in Chapter 4.

Medical reasons

For most people who have trouble with their voices, it is normally due to the way they have used them. However, it is possible that *medical* or even *environmental* reasons may be a cause. Gastroesophageal reflux, allergies, nasal congestion, asthma or exhaustion could lead to problems with the voice.

If a person is having problems with a weak or husky voice, experiencing persistent voice change or repeated sore throats, it is vital that medical help is sought in order that anything 'sinister' can be detected and treated. Such a person should ask a doctor for a referral for an Ear, Nose and Throat check-up, and then to Speech and Language Therapy for voice therapy if necessary.

You can—you must!

Let me close this chapter with the reminder that God has created us and given us the voice, personality and physique that we have. These features are unique and distinctive, and he has a sphere of service prepared for us. Our part, however, is to work on the apparatus with which he has provided us, throwing off bad habits and cultivating new ones, all driven by the burning desire to be mighty instruments in the hand of God.

So let us not shrink back from the task of improving and preserving our voices. It is to the matter of improving our voices that we now turn our attention.

Improving our voices

IN THIS CHAPTER

Posture →
Correct breathing →
Articulation →
Pitching the voice →
Value of physical exercise →

Chapter 3

Endeavour to educate your voice. Grudge no pains or labour in achieving this.

–C. H. Spurgeon, 'On the Voice'

Most preachers claim not to like the sound of their own voice. When listening to a recording of ourselves, we can hardly recognize that it is actually us. This is because, in our heads, we have a perception of what we sound like (we hear our voice's resonance from *inside* our body) and the reality usually disappoints us! We hear some men speak and they seem to be natural orators—in fact, we have to concede that some are 'built' that way and seem to have the physical equipment or perhaps the cultural background that enables them to produce beautiful-sounding speech. Others of us, however, may have to work at it. But the point is that beautiful-sounding speech *is* something that can be acquired. The question really is: Am I bothered enough to *want* to improve my voice?

We noted earlier that A. W. Tozer, who was undoubtedly a man of deep spirituality, had no qualms about seeking to work at the voice that would be used to convey those much-prayed-over messages. In this chapter, therefore, we shall look at the importance of correct posture, breathing, articulation and the pitching of the voice, as well as our inbuilt amplification systems.

Prevention better than cure

My concern is not that we might be eloquent preachers—although true eloquence may well have its place; it is rather that we might be able to proclaim God's truth in a way that maximizes the gifts he has given us.

You may have had the experience of, after purchasing a car, discovering how many other cars of that type are on the road. In the Introduction, I mentioned how shocked I was, after having been told to cease preaching because of voice problems, to discover just how many other preachers had also endured an enforced silence. The vast majority of 'victims' have to hold up their hands and admit that it was all down to either ignorance or neglect of even the most basic principles of voice production and care.

Speaking to young men who hopefully would have decades of ministry ahead of them, Spurgeon bluntly warned, 'One of the surest ways to kill yourself is to speak from the throat instead of the mouth. This misuse of nature will be terribly avenged by her; escape the penalty by avoiding the offence.'[7]

It is surely better to get ourselves into good habits of speaking and thereby avoid trouble further down the line. However, I make no apologies for again pressing the point that this is not merely a health issue, but one of seeking to fulfil our highest potential for the kingdom of God, that he might be pleased to reveal something of his glory to mankind through even these poor stammering lips of ours.

Posture and power

Breath is the energy source behind the voice, and correct breathing is the key to successful voice projection. But our breathing can be radically hindered by bad posture. Poor posture restricts the power and projection of the voice. If a preacher slumps over the pulpit (more likely when reading the Scriptures than in the act of preaching), he constricts the ribcage, thereby losing considerable control over his breathing.

The opposite is equally harmful. If the preacher stands too erect—sergeant-major style—with head right back and shoulders pulled back, the body becomes full of strain and tension, and the throat is constricted.

Standing correctly is important. Stand at ease, with your feet a foot or so apart. Speaking (or singing) when seated is, of course, always more difficult.

Correct breathing

Many a man's voice and ministry could have been saved or prolonged simply by observing the basic rules of good breathing. Far too many preachers breathe too shallowly and therefore run the risk of putting undue pressure upon the throat.

Again, remember: breath is the 'bow' that plays the 'violin string' of the vocal cords. It is your breath that powers your voice, so there must be an ample supply flowing through from the diaphragm.

BREATHING FROM THE DIAPHRAGM

Good breathing requires the use of three sets of muscles: the diaphragm (the muscles below your lungs), the abdomen muscles and the muscles around the ribs.

Have you noticed the way a baby breathes? You will see the tummy rise when he or she inhales, and flatten as he or she exhales. The little one is teaching us the correct way to breathe—using abdominal breathing, which is the most natural and efficient form of breathing. (No wonder that babies have the stamina to cry and keep weary parents awake so effectively!)

Our breathing must be controlled, so avoid:

- taking in too deep a breath of air (as if about to hold your breath underwater), then allowing it to rush out under pressure. This will produce either a strangulated voice or an unusually breathy voice.
- taking too shallow a breath before speaking. This will cause you to compensate for the lack of flow by putting strain on the throat to produce the volume required. The voice will also sound strained or harsh.

It cannot be stressed enough just how important it is to get into good breathing habits and then to maintain these by daily breathing exercises. (See Appendix 1 for breathing exercises.)

Articulation

In Chapter 2, I wrote of the importance of clarity in our speech, and of how our voices are able to carry with less volume simply because of good articulation.

It is the speech organs of the head that turn voice into speech:

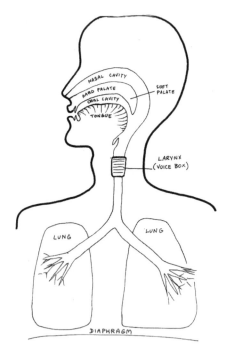

- the tongue
- the lips
- the soft palate—which is at the back of the roof of the mouth and is movable
- the hard palate—which lies in front of the soft palate and is immovable
- the dental ridge—which is just behind the upper front teeth
- the jaw.

As a natural mumbler (perhaps because of lack of self-confidence?), I have always struggled when it comes to clear diction; if you are a *fast* mumbler, double effort must be made. The tongue as well as the lips must be disciplined if clear speech is to be produced—again, exercises are of great benefit. Try reading aloud an expressive poem or some other good literature (remember Tozer and his avid reading of Milton's *Paradise Lost*); what could be better than reading aloud the Scriptures themselves?

The tongue, lips and jaw must move—ventriloquism is out for preachers!

Let's hear Spurgeon on this:

> Take great care of the consonants, enunciate every one of them clearly; they are features and expressions of words. Practise indefatigably till you give every one of the consonants its due; the vowels have a voice of their own, and therefore they can speak for themselves. In all other matters exercise a rigid discipline until you have mastered your voice, and have it in hand like a well-trained steed.[8]

Of course, in pre-amplification days, a preacher was compelled to ensure that every possible effort was made to maximize the sound of his voice so that it could carry and be heard clearly some distance away. We shall look later at the use and abuse of amplification. (See Appendix 1 for articulation exercises.)

Pitching the voice

In the previous chapter, I said that you must find that certain pitch at which your voice operates most comfortably without any straining. Every voice has a natural middle note and it is possible to pitch too high or too low.

Feelings of nervousness, especially at the start of a message, can cause you, through tension in the throat muscles, to pitch higher than is comfortable and natural. On the other hand, it is equally possible not to stretch the voice enough, giving a sound that is dull and monotonous and which is also potentially harmful to your voice.

It is of the utmost importance that you identify your 'middle note', i.e. that particular pitch at which your voice is most comfortable. By shouting out the word 'Hey!' a few times, you should be able to discover it. Also try saying the sounds 'Uh

Huh!' or 'Hmmmm!' (For many people, the pitch will rise the louder they shout.)

Then, of course, the voice will (and must!) vary in pitch. *Inflection* is the 'tune' of the voice. The Welsh have a natural 'sing-song', but we must all learn to cultivate an interesting voice—one that is easy on the ear of the listener and on the throat of the speaker. Again, practising by reading some descriptive literature can be of great benefit.

Helpful as ever, Spurgeon advised his students to

> Lower the voice when suitable even to a whisper; for soft, deliberate, solemn utterances are not only a relief to the ear, but have a great aptitude to reach the heart. Do not be afraid of low keys, for if you throw force into them they are as well heard as the shouts … it is not the loudness of your voice, it is the force which you put into it that is effective.[9]

The important point to remember is that, regardless of the volume used, we must keep within our 'comfort zone' with regard to pitch. This means, of course, that we are constantly to be aware of our voices and able to recognize when we are entering our particular 'danger zone'. This is easier said than done. When God's Word burns in our hearts and we are carried along by our subject and longing to bless those who are listening, then we are most at risk.

We can be released from the inevitable pressure we feel when seeking to affect our hearers by remembering that it is '"Not by might nor by power, but by my Spirit," says the LORD Almighty' (Zech. 4:6). When Spurgeon spoke of 'force', he surely did not preclude that holy force—that unction from heaven that we pray will accompany our frail human efforts each time we speak in Christ's name. Volume and passion are, in themselves alone, powerless when it comes to bringing spiritual change to an eternal soul, and we must ever beware of mistaking perspiration for inspiration!

Exercise—*me*?

Being a preacher of the gospel makes demands physically as well as spiritually. The apostle Paul spoke of being beaten by rods and surviving shipwreck and stoning. He was always on the move and his ministry called for much physical vigour (read 2 Cor. 11:23–27 for a sample). We are called to minister in our pampered twenty-first-century Western culture and are constantly in danger of death by *chairus posterior*, that fatal sitting syndrome that causes the sufferer to shrink from such violent words as 'exercise'! Yet it has been estimated that a half-hour sermon can use up as much energy as eight hours of manual labour. 'Sit-up-and-listen' preaching requires physical strength and stamina, and carrying too much weight will undoubtedly hinder our breathing and voice projection.

Towards the end of his ministry, Paul could speak of 'finishing the race' that God had marked out for him to run. Above all else, he was a preacher, one with a constant awareness that he was an ambassador who had been set apart for this high calling of proclaiming Christ. As the years passed, there was no settling down for this man and, constrained by holy love towards the close of his days as a herald, he urged his young protégé Timothy to 'fan into flame the gift of God, which is in you …' (2 Tim. 1:6).

John Wesley was a man whose life seemed one of perpetual motion. Since the day Christ lit a flame within his heart, he was determined that all his days be used in lighting that flame in the hearts of others. However, despite his seemingly reckless abandonment (covering nearly a quarter of a million miles, mostly on horseback in all weathers, preaching around 40,000 sermons and writing over 200 books[10]), he was vigilant in taking care of the frail frame entrusted to him for this work. This horseback hero gave much time not only to the study of medicine but also in giving medical as well as spiritual advice. He saw no contradiction between striving for holiness and caring for the body. Body as well as soul were at the Master's disposal, and he urged that preachers should avoid carelessness in either area:

> ... Thirdly, Observe all the time the greatest exactness in your regimen or manner of living. Abstain from all mixed, all high seasoned food. Use plain diet, easy of digestion; and this as sparingly as you can, consistent with ease and strength. Drink only water, if it agrees with our stomach; if not, good, clear small beer. Use as much exercise daily in the open air, as you can without weariness. Sup at six or seven on the lightest food; go to bed early, and rise betimes. To persevere with steadiness in this course, is often more than half the cure. Above all, add to the rest, (for it is not labour lost) that old unfashionable medicine, prayer ...[11]

The apostle Paul reminds us of our supreme obligation to keep ourselves fit for ministry spiritually: 'train yourself to be godly' and 'Watch your life and doctrine closely' (1 Tim. 4:7, 16).

The longer we have been preaching, the greater the temptation to be careless; that is why I repeat that there is no more tragic sight under heaven than that of a God-sent preacher who has been silenced through his own folly. Some have disqualified themselves through acts of moral recklessness, but perhaps the vast majority have ceased to preach simply because of physical neglect of some sort or another.

We have an enemy forever working to drive us to extremes, seeking to harm us through carnality or lack of physical awareness on the one hand, or through over-exertion and lack of necessary rest on the other.

Paul did tell us that 'physical training is of *some* value ...'

(1 Tim. 4:8, emphasis added). (See Appendix 1 for exercises for physical flexibility.)

The wear and tear on a preacher's voice can be considerable, and some men are called to areas of ministry that are more demanding on the voice than others. We will look in the final chapter at how best we may preserve our voices, thereby ensuring that we are able faithfully to fulfil the commission entrusted to us.

Preserving our voices

IN THIS CHAPTER
The use of amplification →
Rest →
Ten tips →
The place of prayer and healing →

Chapter 4

Physical training is of some value …

–the apostle Paul

Your voice is like a muscle and needs exercise.

–Billy Graham

The strength of George Whitefield's voice is well documented; it is recorded that he could preach to crowds of up to 40,000 people and be heard distinctly anywhere in such a vast and intense gathering. However, before we say, 'Ah, but he was specially built, a one-off!', we need to remember that John Wesley, who was of short stature and slight build, also addressed such crowds. The argument will not stand that the preachers of past generations were some kind of rare breed of barrel-chested, leather-larynxed natural orators. Surely in those pre-amplification days they had no option but to work on projecting and preserving their voices in order to be heard day after day in such physically demanding times. Doubtless, they were mighty men of God; but they were still just men—frail flesh-and-blood servants of God vulnerable to the very same ailments that threaten to render us lesser men hoarse and helpless.

Use of amplification

The advent of the amplification system is without doubt an enormous blessing, but its abuse has made it a curse for some. Generations have arisen who, because of the awareness that their every breath will be picked up and relayed to the largest audience, have neglected the all-important matter of voice projection and never worked in any way upon their voices.

So how best can we use amplification?

FORGET IT

When using a microphone, you should seek to forget all about it (even if it is tugging at your tie!) and speak in the same voice that seeks to reach the back row as if there were no amplification. The sound engineer should soon be able to gauge the level correct for you. The result should be that the preaching voice sounds natural and does not descend into an intimate whispering 'golf commentary' voice.

BE AWARE OF IT

If you have a fixed pulpit microphone, you need to be aware that, if you move away or step to the side, some in the congregation may miss your words—especially those whose hearing is impaired and are using a loop system.

You should be able to hear your amplified voice. Ideally, the building should have a speaker (fold-back monitor) for the preacher right by the pulpit in order that he hears what the audience hears. If you have difficulty hearing yourself, you will inevitably end up speaking more loudly than necessary.

If possible, get the sound engineer to have much more treble than bass. Too much bass makes the words sound muffled, whereas the treble enables the words to cut through clearly.

The ideal situation is where you are able to test the microphone before the meeting and the sound engineer is able to get the right setting rather than needing to experiment while the message is being preached. (There is nothing worse than 'feedback' that, even if not the kind that breaks out into a deafening howl, is constantly present throughout the message as a distracting whistle.)

Rest

I have sought to show that there is not a more tragic sight in all creation than that of a God-sent preacher who is forced to be silent. But if there are not times of *voluntary* silence—that all-vital rest that nature demands our voices to have—then trouble is bound to follow.

We can be strangely inconsistent creatures when it comes to

this area of rest—quite capable of dispensing pastoral advice on adequate rest and refreshment to others, but somehow failing to apply that same principle to our own lives and practices.

The God who created all things in six days and then rested on the seventh clearly lays down for us a pattern we ignore at our peril. We do not serve a God who is unmindful of our human frailties but who throughout the Scriptures continues to remind us of this pattern of work and rest. Both work and rest are important; God does not see rest as time wasted.

On a number of occasions, it has taken loving rebukes from concerned and respected fellow ministers to bring me to my senses, pointing out the long-term consequences of ignoring not only God's dealings in providence, but also the pattern for rest he has given in his Word.

This folly has been likened to that of an old farmer who is too busy to stop and sharpen his scythe and so continues ineffectively with a blunt instrument; or that of the fisherman who is too busy to take time to mend his nets, thereby failing to bring in the harvest of the sea he might otherwise have had.

There is a reason why we struggle in this area, of course. We are men with an all-important message and calling, and this 'fire in the bones' constrains and drives us throughout the years. We continue to 'preach the Word' despite seasons of discouragement and, at times, even fierce opposition. It is no wonder, then, that we refuse to be stopped by 'a little throat problem', and it's so easy to fail to recognize that such a problem is no small matter.

D. L. Moody was once due to visit several of the larger cities in England and afterwards hold an eight-day mission at Spurgeon's Metropolitan Tabernacle, but, leading up to this, he suffered from throat trouble that caused him some considerable anxiety.[12] We can pour out much time, energy and prayer planning important schedules and events for the kingdom of God, yet forget that we are but frail mortals. It is so easy for preachers to be driven by a heavy agenda and ignore the early signs that our voices may be in need of care and attention. Proper rest earlier on could save much enforced rest later.

Ten tips for caring for the voice

Various exercises are provided in Appendix 1, but let us first look briefly at a few tips to help us to take proper care of our vital 'tool of the trade'.

1. WARM UP THE VOICE BEFORE SPEAKING

Watch how the athlete warms up his or her muscles before that all-important event to prevent injury, or how the singer warms up his or her voice before taking the stage for the performance. The preacher dare not think he is able to get the best out of his voice without similar preparation before the demanding act of preaching; it can be helpful to think of ourselves as 'vocal athletes'. Remember also that during a break in your regular speaking ministry—e.g. a holiday or sabbatical—the voice still needs to be exercised. The preacher who preaches wisely on a daily basis is less likely to have trouble than the one who preaches just once a week. (See Appendix 1 for warming up exercises.)

2. AVOID FREQUENT COUGHING AND CLEARING OF THE THROAT

Frequent coughing and clearing of the throat can do much harm, as this causes the sensitive, curtain-like vocal cords in the voice box to bang against each other, and damage can be done to the vocal tissue. Instead of clearing the throat, try a silent 'he-he-he' giggle. Swallowing hard a couple of times and sipping water also help.

3. KEEP THE VOCAL TRACT LUBRICATED

We need to be drinking much water. Although water taken during preaching may be of temporary benefit, the body needs to be well hydrated already through a good amount of water taken beforehand (6–8 glasses of water is a recommended minimum). Bear in mind that drinks containing caffeine (e.g. tea and coffee) will dehydrate you. If you find that your throat is dry and you have no access to water, swallow saliva as a stopgap measure.

4. REST WHEN TIRED OR UNWELL

There are certain periods in ministry when we are at a low and are not only physically but perhaps also mentally and emotionally drained. These are always dangerous times for us, made all the more perilous because of the often subtle and gradual descent into these conditions. Rest really is a healer and we must have the sense to rest our voices when tell-tale signs are showing, for example, a sore throat or a strained and ragged voice. To continue in such a condition will only cause the situation to deteriorate and could possibly cause long-term damage. Anaesthetic lozenges and sprays only succeed in masking the problem.

5. SEEK TO AVOID TENSION

Because we are men with a God-given burden, we will have a right nervousness that is to be expected by those who are about to deliver the Word of God. But remember that bodily tension is an enemy to preaching, as it badly affects the posture and breathing. The more relaxed the preacher is, the less risk he faces of straining his voice. It is wise to ensure that there are no church business discussions or decisions needing to be made prior to going into the pulpit! These are normally the real culprits of that unhealthy and unwanted tension.

6. ENSURE THE ROOM IS WELL VENTILATED

Hot, airless churches are a curse to the preacher for a number of reasons. A hot, dry atmosphere not only aids in sending our listeners to sleep (although we must take *some* responsibility for this!), but it also prematurely dries out the preacher's throat.

7. SING BEFORE THE MESSAGE

This can be helpful or unhelpful. If you are able to sing carefully (from the diaphragm), it can be useful for warming up (not forgetting to worship!), but if the singing is adding to the strain on your voice, it is best to abstain. The danger occurs when the sound engineer has switched off your microphone and you are unable to hear your own voice because of the congregation. This results in you unknowingly singing more loudly than is wise.

8. AVOID CERTAIN DRINKS AND FOOD BEFORE SPEAKING

Dairy products have the effect of increasing the production of mucus, which can take the edge off your voice. Avoid things like milky drinks, chocolate, cheese and so on directly before speaking.

Eating spicy foods the night before can also be harmful, as acid from the stomach can lie on the vocal cords all night, affecting the way you sound in the morning.

9. BE CAREFUL AFTER THE MEETING

Often the greatest strain on our voices can be when attempting to speak to someone in an after-church setting, where you are competing with the background noise of loud chatter and teacups. This is compounded in a room with bare walls and lots of echo. Be very careful not to strain the voice here. The danger is that we feel that we have 'done the business' and can now relax. It is now that we can be off guard and lapse into shallower breathing and lazier voice production. The rule is: when it is noisy, don't speak more loudly, but articulate more clearly.

10. TAKE CARE IN AN OPEN-AIR SITUATION

Here you have no walls or ceiling to enable the sound to bounce back to you, so you have no means of judging how the sound is carrying. If at all possible, find a spot where there is a building on at least one side of you; this will be of help. If not, there is a great danger of speaking more loudly at a sustained level than is comfortable, thereby straining the voice. Also, the greater the background noise, the greater the risk of doing harm to the voice.

When trouble strikes!

What are we to do when we arrive at that painful conclusion that something is wrong?

The term 'vocal abuse' may sound a little extreme, but it does accurately describe what has led to the problem encountered—that is, improper use of the voice, such as speaking too loudly or at an unhealthy pitch for too long and failing to rest when necessary. *It is vital to understand that such misuse can damage the vocal cords and, if not heeded, can lead to permanent damage.*

Fortunately, most disorders that come as a result of vocal abuse are reversible. Let us briefly consider the main ones common to preachers and public speakers.

Vocal cord nodules and polyps

Vocal cord nodules and polyps are benign growths on the vocal cord. A vocal polyp is similar to a vocal nodule but is softer, like a blister compared with a callus. A polyp normally occurs on one side of the vocal cord, whereas nodules appear on both sides, typically at the midpoint, and directly face each other.

- Symptoms—the voice becomes breathy, low-pitched, hoarse (perhaps chronically), tired, 'scratchy' and unreliable.
- Treatment—seek medical help.

Some respond well to rest and voice therapy alone, while others require surgery.

Contact ulcers

A contact ulcer is an ulcerated sore which appears on the vocal cord and is caused by using too much force in speaking. The excessive force causes the vocal cords to 'bang together', wearing away the tissue near the cartilage of the larynx.

- Symptoms—pain in the throat (especially while speaking), 'scratchy' voice, voice tires easily.

• Treatment—seek medical help.

Avoid anything that is causing harm to the larynx, and rest the voice. A speech therapist is invaluable, and learning good vocal techniques will prove to be of lifelong benefit as bad habits are shed and good ones learned.

The place of prayer and healing

Much that has been written in these pages has been with the aim of making us aware of what *we* are to do, as preachers, in order to keep our voices healthy. However, we dare not neglect our responsibility heavenwards when we experience problems, nor be unmindful of God's providential dealings at such times. Let me cite just two cases in order to remind us never to leave God's intervention out of our reckoning.

Prayer: Hywel Griffiths, Bridgend

Hywel Griffiths was a predecessor of mine at Litchard Mission Church, Bridgend, South Wales, and was reckoned to be a powerful and anointed Welsh preacher. Prior to his acceptance of the pastorate at Litchard in the mid-1940s, he had worked as a miner in a colliery. His ministry at Litchard was put in jeopardy because of ill health after contracting tuberculosis of the throat which, in those days, still claimed the lives of many.

After an operation in the University Hospital of Wales, Cardiff, the doctor said that Griffiths would never speak again above a whisper.

However, every week, prayer was passionately offered up by the saints for Mr Griffiths' voice to be strengthened, claiming the promise from the lips of the Lord Jesus: 'Therefore I tell you, whatever you ask for in prayer, believe that you have received it, and it will be yours' (Mark 11:24).

Prayer was answered and eventually his voice returned with such power that he was able not only to preach indoors, but also to speak with volume and clarity in the open-air meetings that he regularly held. The doctor acknowledged that it was a miracle, and Hywel Griffiths continued to exercise his powerful ministry in South Wales until his death in 1972.[13]

Providence: Charles Simeon, Cambridge

Charles Simeon was vicar of Holy Trinity Church in Cambridge for fifty-four years and, despite much opposition, established a ministry that even today is seen as a focal point of evangelicalism in England. However, in 1807, after twenty-five years of ministry, his voice failed and he could speak no more loudly than a whisper; after preaching, he remarked that he felt 'more like one dead than alive'. This dreadful situation lasted for thirteen years, until he was sixty years of age. But this seemingly hopeless situation was turned around remarkably, and in such a way that Simeon was convinced it could only be explained in terms of God's personal dealings with him.

He told of how once, as he was crossing the English border to visit Scotland, he was 'almost as perceptibly revived in strength as the woman was after she had touched the hem of our Lord's garment'. His view of this restoration was simply that it was the providential hand of God at work in his life and he could trace it back beyond the voice problem to plans that he had made to live an active life of service up to the age of sixty and then afterwards take a little ease. Now, however, it seemed as if his Master was saying to him:

> I laid you aside, because you entertained with satisfaction the thought of resting from your

> labour; but now you have arrived at the very period you had promised yourself that satisfaction, and have determined instead to spend your strength for me to the latest hour in your life, I have doubled, trebled, quadrupled your strength, that you may execute your desire on a more extended plan.[14]

Indeed, Charles Simeon continued to exercise his influential ministry for a further sixteen years, until his death in 1836 at the age of seventy-seven. The point I make simply is twofold:

- Even though we seek medical advice and help, we must never neglect faith-filled, expectant prayer.
- We must always remember that we are in the hands of a sovereign God, who is working all things for the good of those who love him and who have been called for his own purpose and eternal glory. Or, as a godly old elder at a church where I served in Wales used to say at times (with a wink to his often unwise young pastor), 'Not only the steps, but also the *stops* of a good man are ordered by the Lord!'

Exercises: Breathing, physical flexibility, warming up, articulation

by Lulu Housman, B.Sc., ADVS (Advanced Diploma in Voice Studies), Voice Specialist in the Speech and Language Therapy department at West Middlesex University Hospital (Hounslow Primary Care Trust)

Breathing exercises

In case any feel self-conscious regarding these exercises, I've worked with students at the London Academy of Music and Dramatic Art (LAMDA) for many years and have found that these students will try most things if asked, especially if they will prove to be of benefit to them!

Try to do the following exercises with a lightness in your heart—there is no need to criticize yourself or tell yourself off. It's better to think in terms of finding out what you can do and experimenting for yourself. Breathing exercises both relax you and give you energy.

- Stand with your feet shoulder-width apart. Relax mentally, and sense your spine feeling tall and your shoulders relaxed and feeling wide and open across your chest. Imagine that your head is like a balloon filled with helium which can float towards the ceiling.
- Check that your neck feels free by making tiny circles in the air with the tip of your nose—to the left and then to the right.
- Breathe in through your nose and slowly reach up to the ceiling with your hands, stretching your fingertips as far as they can go. Then slowly breathe out, bringing your arms and hands down to your sides. Do this slowly five times.
- To improve your breath capacity and stamina, repeat this exercise, mentally counting slowly to ten as you breathe in and then again as you breathe out. Then gradually increase the length of your out breath from ten upwards. Find out your limit!
- The next step is gently to say 's' as you exhale slowly. See if you can do this for about twenty seconds (twenty–twenty-five seconds is the average for an adult, but this

reduces as we get older). You can do this without using your arms. Just rest if you overdo it and feel dizzy.

CHECK THAT YOU ARE USING YOUR DIAPHRAGM

Some relaxing music may help as you do this one:

- When you have five minutes to spare, lie down on your back on the floor with a thick book under your head and your knees bent and pointing to the ceiling. (This is called the semi-supine position; it is a marvellous position for working on the voice.)
- Place one hand on the upper chest and one around your

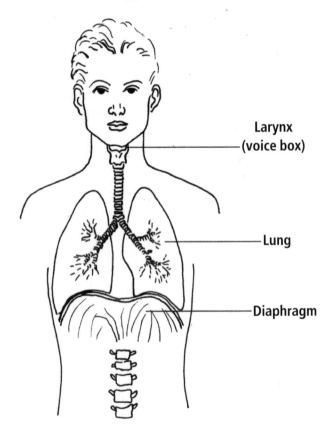

Larynx (voice box)

Lung

Diaphragm

tummy button. Breathe slowly and evenly, making sure that only your lower hand is moving up and down. If your upper chest is doing the work, put a heavy book on your stomach and practise pushing it up towards the ceiling. Keep the breathing slow and even, and try not to inhale too deeply at this stage.

Running, cycling and swimming all help with breathing.

Physical flexibility

SHOULDER TURNS

- Stand with your feet apart. Keep the back of your knees soft and unlocked. Make the spine tall and your head floating away to the ceiling.
- Slowly rotate your shoulders five times. They need to go forward together, up towards your ears (try to pull them above your ears!), then down and back. Try to get the shoulder blades to touch on the way down.

LIFTS AND DROPS

- Raise your shoulders together, squeezing them hard, and then let them go suddenly. Let gravity take over—don't guide them down.
- Repeat this seven times.

NECK

- Face the front and turn your head to look over your shoulder—hold this for ten seconds.
- Then slowly look up to the ceiling and down to the floor. Turn your head back to the front and repeat with your other shoulder.

SPINE

- Stand with your feet apart.

- Drop your chin to your chest and let it feel heavy. Then let the weight of it lead you down towards the floor, so that you hang over, bent in half at the waist. Keep the back of the knees soft all the time, not locked. You'll find that you can feel the lower ribs moving as you breathe in and out.
- Stay there for a short while and keep your neck completely free. Sway a little from side to side.
- Then slowly unwind again so that your head is the very last to appear. Let your spine feel tall, your shoulders relaxed. It's very important that you keep your head down towards your chest as you slowly come up, and only raise your head at the very end.

Warming-up exercises
Warming up the voice makes all the difference!

HUMMING

- Gently hum several times on a comfortable note—neither very high nor very low. Feel the vibrations on your lips and across your cheekbones. Then choose a comfortable low note and glide the note upwards five times towards your top range—but without strain.
- Then glide from low to high and high to low, sounding like a siren. This can be done quite gently as you are just warming up. (Remember to keep your shoulders relaxed and low, and to breathe as if to your stomach.)
- Add to this by intoning on one note, keeping a relaxed tongue and jaw. If these are too tense, the sound is stopped from coming out; so separate your teeth and make sure your tongue is lying neutrally in your mouth, like a rug on the floor:
Mer Mer Mer Mer Mer
Mah Mah Mah Mah Mah

Meh Meh Meh Meh Meh

- Then, as if you're arriving through the front door and calling out in a 'singy' kind of way: '*Mum I'm home!*' '*Mum I'm home!*' '*Mum I'm home!*' '*Mum I'm home!*'
- Feel the vibrations forward in the cheekbones or lips. (Some people feel more vibrations in the chest.)
- Then change the sound to 'EE'. It can help to smile at the same time—this helps the larynx to remain open and wide rather than closed and tight.
- Now change the sound to 'NG': glides from high to low (five times) and sirens (five times).

After a few minutes, your voice will feel fuller and more resonant. The vocal cords contain muscles that respond well to being used and stretched.

Intonation

- Take a simple sentence and repeat it several times, putting emphasis on a different word each time. For example, take 'The sun is shining; there are no clouds in the sky.'
  *The **sun** is shining; there are no clouds in the sky.*
  *The sun is **shining**; there are no clouds in the sky.*
  *The sun is shining; there **are** no clouds in the sky.*
  *The sun is shining; there are **no** clouds in the sky.*
- You've got the idea. Although it might seem a bit odd at first, it's a useful exercise for us to hear different patterns from the ones we normally follow. Try to connect with what you're saying. Visualize the images and commit to saying it.
- Here are some more sentences to try (try some sentences of your own, too):
  I love these wild, wet, windy days in autumn.
  Let's go out for a long walk to pick blackberries.
  The traffic this morning was dreadful!

Where have I seen you before?
It's easy to see why he loves her.

We need to remind ourselves to connect emotionally and to mean what we say. If you don't believe in what you're saying, you can't commit to it.

Poetry or reading sentences from a favourite author might be a better place for you to start. Reading aloud from a book where several characters are having a dialogue is an excellent way to find more variety in your voice. Each character has its unique voice. (I'm particularly fond of *Winnie the Pooh* by A. A. Milne!)

ARTICULATION

- Have a good yawn and stretch and sigh. (It's like aerobics for your throat!) The best yawns are when tears come to your eyes.
- Massage your jaw, face and scalp in a gentle, invigorating way.
- Move your lips, tongue and jaw around for several seconds as if you are chewing a very sticky toffee.
- Take a deep breath and make lots of 'ge ge ge ge' sounds with the back of your tongue, like the sound of sherry being poured from a bottle. Start on a slightly higher note than the one you end on.
- Roll your tongue 'rrrrrrrrrrrrrrrrrrrrr' on a low-pitched note as if you are frustrated about something or someone!
- This is a classic articulation exercise:
  Bah Bay Bee Bay Bah Baw Boo Baw
  Pah Pay Pee Pay Pah Paw Poo Paw
  Dah Day Dee Day Dah Daw Doo Daw
  Tah Tay Tee Tay Tah Taw Too Taw
  Lah Lay Lee Lay Lah Law Loo Law
  Nah Nay Nee Nay Nah Naw Noo Naw

Sah Say See Say Sah Saw Soo Saw
- You can then add any consonant you like to the sequence, which goes like this:
  ah ay ee ay ah aw oo aw ('aw' as in 'paw')
  G, K, Ch, J, R, W, Ch, Y
- Try putting the consonant after the vowels (this is where we all tend to forget to make the effort, so clarity is lost as we fade away at the ends of words or sentences). So here's how it goes:
  AhB ayB eeB ayB ahB awB ooB awB
  AhP ayP eeP ayP ahP awP ooP awP
  AhT ayT eeT ayT ahT awT ooT awT
  AhD ayD eeD ayD ahD awD ooD awD
- Then, of course, you can make things harder by combining consonants into clusters. Try:
  st bl tr gr fl
  and:
  str kst
- I'm also fond of the Peter Piper tongue-twister, partly because you have to work out what is going on. It's easier if you find words to emphasize. Have a go, starting slowly and clearly and building up your speed:
  Peter Piper picked a peck of pickled pepper.
  If Peter Piper picked a peck of pickled pepper,
  Where's the peck of pickled pepper Peter Piper picked?
  Keep the consonants bouncy and energetic to give the lips and tongue a workout.

Try to keep all these exercises light and experimental. Laugh a lot, as much as you like—it's wonderful for the throat.

Three important reminders:

- Stand up tall.
- Breathe in.
- Speak up and out.

➡ Look after your voice

Drink plenty of water—it makes the vocal cords more efficient; avoid too much tea and coffee when you have to speak for a while. If you are worried about your voice, ask your doctor to refer you to your local Ear, Nose and Throat department, which can then refer you on to your local Speech and Language Therapist who specializes in voice disorders.

A physiology of voice

by Martyn Leggett, MB, BS, FRCS (ORL-HNS),
Associate Specialist in Ear, Nose and Throat Surgery
at Poole Hospital (Dorset Primary Care Trust)

Introduction

In addition to neurological pathways of speech, the production of voice requires the integration of three mechanisms:

- bellows
- vibrating mechanism
- resonators.

BELLOWS

This involves the production of a high-pressure column of air from the lungs and is achieved by chest and abdominal muscle contractions. In order for pressure to rise significantly, there must be an obstruction to the flow of air, which is achieved by closing the vocal cords.

VIBRATING MECHANISM

This is the true function of the cords and is thought to be similar to a reed instrument. Once the pressure reaches a certain level, the cords begin to vibrate. The alternating opening and closing of the glottis produces a vibrating column of air, which can be modified by the resonators.

RESONATORS

These comprise the thorax, pharynx, mouth, nose and sinuses. The tone emanating from the larynx is weak and non-resonant. The resonators give richness and quality to the voice. The walls of the resonators are partly fixed and partly mobile, namely, the tongue, lips and cheeks. They increase volume, reinforce overtones and give the voice individuality by producing a complex waveform.

Thus voice production is a complex integration of the muscles of phonation, articulation and resonance.

Larynx

The larynx is composed of a skeletal structure (predominantly cartilage) and muscles, which move the cartilages in relation to each other. The vocal cords are attached to the thyroid cartilage at the front and the arytenoid at the back. The arytenoids sit on top of the cricoid cartilage. Thus movement of the cricoid cartilage in relation to the thyroid cartilage will affect the tension of the vocal cords, and movement of the arytenoids on the cricoid cartilage will affect the horizontal position of the vocal cords.

Vocal cord

The vocal cord comprises a ligament and covering lining. The lining has a (epithelial) layer and a sub-epithelial layer. The integrity of the sub-epithelial layer is of crucial importance. This is not fixed rigidly to the ligament but permits gliding over the ligament and alteration of shape of the cord during phonation. This, while essential for proper functioning, makes the cord susceptible to damage. The main causes of damage are trauma from misuse, dehydration, smoking and irradiation. The effects of damage are formation of nodules (usually at the point of maximum movement of the cord and therefore maximum force of contact) and degeneration of the sub-epithelial layer resulting in polyp formation. Proper care of the voice should prevent these from occurring.

Phonation

The vocal cords are closed and tensed by muscles both within and without the larynx. With the cords closed, the rising pressure causes the cord edge to roll upwards and outwards; in other words, the area of contact is forced apart by pressure from below.

The vibration created may involve the whole length of the cord or just the front portion.

The lower the pitch, the longer the period of contact between the cords, and vice versa.

The act of opening and closing the cords results in the production of rhythmical, short columns of air, which can be modified by the resonators.

Pitch variation

Pitch is a result of the frequency of the oscillations of the cords and is determined by the length, tension and shape of the vocal cord. The shape can vary from a thin cord with a sharp edge to a cord which is thick, rounded and has a flat edge. An increase in pitch results from increasing tension and change of shape of the cord. Low-frequency sounds are produced by broad cords of low tension vibrating along the full length.

Normal speech is the result of changes in the tension and shape of the cords, but singing produces an extra dimension as the cords actually *lengthen* as pitch rises, requiring an extra increase in tension.

Volume

This is predominantly due to the pressure generated below in the vocal cords. But pressure also affects pitch. Increasing volume results in slight increase in pitch for which singers are trained to compensate.

Control mechanisms

There are a number of mechanisms which contribute to control, particularly pre-tuning, whereby all muscles are set at the correct tension before phonation begins, and also acoustic auto-monitoring, whereby what the speaker hears modulates voice production.

Conclusion

The production of voice is a complex system involving the central nervous system and co-ordination of many muscles around the larynx. It can therefore be no surprise that minor changes in one part of the system can have significant effects on the quality of voice production and, consequently, that those who rely on their voices should ensure that they properly use them.

'On the voice'

by C. H. Spurgeon (from
Lectures To My Students)

Our first rule with regard to the voice would be, *do not think too much about it*, for recollect the sweetest voice is nothing without something to say, and however well it may be managed, it will be like a well-driven cart with nothing in it, unless you convey by it important and seasonable truths to your people. Demosthenes was doubtless right, in giving a first, second and third place to a good delivery; but of what value will that be if a man has nothing to deliver? A man with a surpassingly excellent voice who is destitute of a well-informed head, and an earnest heart, will be 'a voice crying in the wilderness'; or, to use Plutarch's expression, '*Vox et praeterea nihil.*' Such a man may shine in the choir, but he is useless in the pulpit. Whitefield's voice, without his heart-power, would have left no more lasting effects upon his hearers than Paganini's fiddle. You are not singers but preachers: your voice is but a secondary matter; do not be *fops* with it, or puling [whining] invalids over it, as so many are. A trumpet need not be made of silver, a ram's-horn will suffice; but it must be able to endure rough usage, for trumpets are for war's conflicts, not for the drawing-rooms of fashion.

On the other hand, *do not think too little of your voice*, for its excellence may greatly conduce to the result which you hope to produce. Plato, in confessing the power of eloquence, mentions the tone of the speaker. 'So strongly,' says he, 'does the speech and the tone of the orator ring in my ears, that scarcely in the third or fourth day, do I recollect myself, and perceive where on the earth I am; and for awhile I am willing to believe myself living in the isles of the blessed.' Exceedingly precious truths may be greatly matted by being delivered in monotonous tones. I once heard a most esteemed minister, who mumbled sadly, compared to 'a humble bee in a pitcher', a vulgar metaphor no doubt, but so exactly descriptive, that it brings to my mind the droning sound at this instant most distinctly, and reminds me of the parody upon Gray's Elegy:

> Now fades the glimmering subject from the sight,
> And all the air a sleepy stillness holds,
> Save where the parson hums his droning flight,
> And drowsy tinklings lull the slumb'ring folds.

What a pity that a man who from his heart delivered doctrines of undoubted value, in language the most appropriate, should commit ministerial suicide by harping on one string, when the Lord had given him an instrument of many strings to play upon! Alas! alas! for that dreary voice, it hummed and hummed like a mill-wheel to the same unmusical turn, whether its owner spake of heaven or hell, eternal life or everlasting wrath. It might be, by accident, a little louder or softer, according to the length of the sentence, but its tone was still the same, a dreary waste of sound, a howling wilderness of speech in which there was no possible relief, no variety, no music, nothing but horrible sameness.

When the wind blows through the Aeolian harp, it swells through all the chords, but the heavenly wind, passing through some men, spends itself upon one string, and that, for the most part, the most out of tune of the whole. Grace alone could enable hearers to edify under the drum—drum—drum of some divines. I think an impartial jury would bring in a verdict of justifiable slumbering in many cases where the sound emanating from the preacher lulls to sleep by its reiterated note. Dr Guthrie charitably traces the slumbers of a certain Scotch congregation to bad ventilation in the meeting-house; this has something to do with it, but a bad condition of the valves of the preacher's throat might be a still more potent cause. Brethren, in the name of everything that is sacred, ring the whole chime in your steeple, and do not dun your people with the ding-dong of one poor cracked bell.

When you do pay attention to the voice, *take care not to fall into the habitual and common affectations of the present day.* Scarcely one man in a dozen in the pulpit talks like a man.

This affectation is not confined to Protestants, for the Abbé Mullois remarks, 'Everywhere else, men speak: they speak at the bar and the tribune; but they no longer speak in the pulpit, for there we only meet with a factitious and artificial language, and a false tone. This style of speaking is only tolerated in the church, because, unfortunately, it is so general there; elsewhere it would not be endured. What would be thought of a man who should converse in a similar way in a drawing-room? He would certainly provoke many a smile. Some time ago there was a warder at the Pantheon—a good sort of fellow in his way— who, in enumerating the beauties of the monument, adopted precisely the tone of many of our preachers, and never failed thereby to excite the hilarity of the visitors, who were as much amused with his style of address as with the objects of interest which he pointed out to them. A man who has not a natural and true delivery, should not be allowed to occupy the pulpit; from thence, at least, everything that is false should be summarily banished ... In these days of mistrust everything that is false should be set aside; and the best way of correcting one's self in that respect, as regards preaching, is frequently to listen to certain monotonous and vehement preachers. We shall come away in such disgust, and with such a horror of their delivery, that we shall prefer condemning ourselves to silence rather than imitate them. The instant you abandon the natural and the true, you forego the right to be believed, as well as the right of being listened to.' You may go all round, to church and chapel alike, and you will find that by far the larger majority of our preachers have a holy tone for Sundays. They have one voice for the parlour and the bedroom, and quite another tone for the pulpit; so that, if not double-tongued sinfully, they certainly are so literally. The moment some men shut the pulpit door, they leave their own personal manhood behind them, and become as official as the parish beadle. There they might almost boast with the Pharisee, that they are not as other men are, although it would be blasphemy to thank God for it. No longer are they carnal and speak as men, but a whine, a broken hum-haw, an *ore rotundo*, or some other graceless mode of noise-making, is adopted, to prevent all suspicion of being natural and speaking out of the abundance of the heart. When that gown is once on, how often does it prove to be the shroud of the man's true self, and the effeminate emblem of officialism!

There are two or three modes of speech which I dare say you will recognize as having frequently heard. That dignified, doctoral, inflated, bombastic style, which I just now called the *ore rotundo*, is not quite so common now as it used to be, but it is still admired by some. [Unfortunately, the Lecturer could not here be reported by any known form of letter-press, as he proceeded to read a hymn with a round, rolling, swelling voice.] When a reverend gentleman was once blowing off steam in this way, a man in the aisle said he thought the preacher 'had swallowed a dumpling', but another whispered, 'No, Jack, he ain't swaller'd un; he's got un in his mouth a-wobblin'.' I can imagine Dr Johnson talking in that fashion, at Bolt Court; and from men to whom it is natural it rolls with Olympian grandeur, but in the pulpit away for ever with all imitation of it; if it comes naturally, well and good, but to mimic it is treason to common decency: indeed, all mimicry is in the pulpit near akin to an unpardonable sin.

There is another style, at which I beseech you not to laugh. [Giving another illustration.] A method of enunciation said to be very lady-like, mincing, delicate, servant-girlified, dawdling, Dundrearyish, I know not how else to describe it. We have, most of us, had the felicity of hearing these, or some others, of the extensive genus of falsettos, high-stilts and affectations. I have heard many different varieties, from the fulness of the Johnsonian to the thinness of the little genteel whisper; from the roaring of the Bulls of Bashan up to the chip, chip, chip of a chaffinch. I have been able to trace some of our brethren to their forefathers—I mean their ministerial forefathers, from whom they first of all gathered these heavenly, melodious, sanctified, in every way beautiful, but I must honestly add detestable modes of speech. The undoubted order of their oratorical pedigree is as follows: Chip, which was the son of Lisp, which was the son of Simper, which was the son of Dandy, which was the son of Affectation; or Wobbler, which was the son of Grandiose, which was the son of Pomposity, the same was the father of many sons. Understand, that where even these horrors of sound are natural, I do not condemn them—let every creature speak in its own tongue; but the fact is, that in nine cases out of ten, these sacred brogues, which I hope will soon be dead languages, are unnatural and strained. I am persuaded that these tones and semitones and monotones are Babylonian, that they are not at all the Jerusalem dialect; for the Jerusalem dialect has this one distinguishing mark, that it is a man's own mode of speech, and is the same out of the pulpit as it is in it. Our friend of the affected *ore rotundo* school was never known to talk out of the pulpit as he does in, or to say in the parlour in the same tone which he uses in the pulpit, 'Will you be so good as to give me another cup of tea; I take sugar, if you please.' He would make himself ludicrous if he did so, but the pulpit is to be favoured with the scum of his voice, which the parlour would not tolerate. I maintain that the best notes a man's voice is capable of should be given to the proclamation of the gospel, and these are such as nature teaches him to use in earnest conversation. Ezekiel served his Master with his most musical and melodious powers, so that the Lord said, 'Thou art unto them as a very lovely song of one that hath a pleasant voice, and can play well on an instrument.' Although, this, alas! was of no use to Israel's hard heart, as nothing will be but the Spirit of God, yet it well became the prophet to deliver the word of the Lord in the best style of voice and manner.

In the next place, *if you have any idiosyncrasies of speech, which are disagreeable to the ear, correct them, if possible.* ['Take care of anything awkward or affected either in your gesture, phrase, or pronunciation'—John Wesley.] It is admitted that this is much more easy for the teacher to inculcate than for you to practise. Yet to young men in the morning of their ministry, the difficulty is not insuperable. Brethren from the country have a flavour of their rustic diet in their mouths, reminding us irresistibly of the calves of Essex, the swine of Berkshire or the runts of Suffolk. Who can mistake the Yorkshire or Somersetshire dialects, which are not merely provincial pronunciations, but tones also? It would be difficult to discover the cause, but the fact is clear enough, that in some counties of England men's throats seem to be furred up, like long-used tea-kettles, and in others, they ring like brass music, with a vicious metallic sound. Beautiful these variations of nature may be in their season and place, but my taste has never been able to appreciate them. A sharp discordant squeak, like a rusty pair of scissors, is to be got rid of at all hazards; so also is a thick, inarticulate utterance in which no word is complete, but nouns, adjectives and verbs are made into a kind of hash. Equally objectionable is that ghostly speed in which a man talks without using his lips, ventriloquizing most horribly: sepulchral tones may fit a man to be an undertaker, but Lazarus is not called out of his grave by hollow moans. One of the surest ways to kill yourself is to speak from the throat instead of the mouth. This misuse of nature will be terribly avenged by her; escape the penalty by avoiding the offence. It may be well in this place to urge you, as soon as you detect yourself interposing hum-haw pretty plentifully in your discourse, to purge yourself of the insinuating but ruinous habit at once. There is no need whatever for it, and although those who are now its victims may never be able to break the chain, you, who are beginners in oratory, must scorn to wear the galling yoke. It is even needful to say, open your mouths when you speak, for much of inarticulate mumbling is the result of keeping the mouth half closed. It is not in vain that the evangelists have written of our Lord, 'He *opened his mouth* and taught them.' Open wide the doors from which such goodly truth is to march forth. Moreover, brethren, avoid the use of the nose as an organ of speech, for the best authorities are agreed that it is intended to smell with. Time was, when the nasal twang was the correct thing, but in this degenerate age you had better obey the evident suggestion of nature, and let the mouth keep to its work without the interference of the olfactory instrument. Should an American student be present he must excuse my pressing this remark upon his attention. Abhor the practice of some men, who will not bring out the letter 'r'; such a habit is 'vewy wuinous and wediculous, vewy wetched and wepwehensible'. Now and then a brother has the felicity to possess a most winning and delicious lisp. This is perhaps among the least of evils, *where the brother himself is little and winning*, but it would ruin any being who aimed at manliness and force. I can scarcely conceive of Elijah lisping to Ahab, or Paul prettily chipping his words on Mars' Hill. There may be a peculiar pathos about a weak and watery eye, and a faltering style; we will go further, and admit that where these are the result of intense passion, they are sublime; but some possess them by birth, and use them rather too freely: it is, to say the least, unnecessary for you to imitate them. Speak as educated nature suggests to you, and you will do well; but let it be educated, and not raw, rude, uncultivated nature. Demosthenes took, as you know, unbounded pains with his voice, and Cicero, who was naturally weak, made a long journey into Greece to correct his manner of speaking. With far nobler themes, let us not be less ambitious to excel. 'Deprive me of everything else,' says Gregory of Nazianzen, 'but leave me eloquence, and I shall never regret the voyages which I have made in order to study it.'

Always speak so as to be heard. I know a man who weighs sixteen stone, and ought to be able to be heard half-a-mile, who is so gracelessly indolent, that in his small place of worship you can scarcely hear him in the front of the gallery. What is the use of a preacher whom men cannot hear? Modesty should lead a voiceless man to give place to others who are more fitted for the work of proclaiming the messages of the King. Some men are loud enough, but they are not distinct, their words overlap each other, play at leap-frog, or trip each other up. Distinct utterance is far more important than wind-power. Do give a word a fair chance, do not break its back in your vehemence, or run it off its legs in your haste. It is hateful to hear a big fellow mutter and whisper when his lungs are quite strong enough for the loudest speech; but at the same time, let a man shout ever so lustily, he will not be well heard unless he learns to push his words forward with due space between. To speak too slowly is miserable work, and subjects active-minded hearers to the disease called the 'horrors'. It is impossible to hear a man who crawls along at a mile an hour. One word today and one tomorrow is a kind of slow-fire which martyrs only could enjoy.

Excessively rapid speaking, tearing and raving into utter rant, is quite as inexcusable; it is not, and never can be powerful, except with idiots, for it turns what should be an army of words into a mob, and most effectually drowns the sense in floods of sound. Occasionally, one hears an infuriated orator of indistinct utterance, whose impetuosity hurries him on to such a confusion of sounds, that at a little distance one is reminded of Lucan's lines:

> Her gabbling tongue a muttering tone confounds,
> Discordant and unlike to human sounds;
> It seem'd of dogs the bark, of wolves the howl,
> The doleful screeching of the midnight owl;
> The hiss of snakes, the hungry lion's roar,
> The bound of billows beating on the shore;
> The groan of winds among the leafy wood,
> And burst of thunder from the rending cloud!
> 'Twas these, all these in one.

It is an infliction not to be endured twice, to hear a brother who mistakes perspiration for inspiration, tear along like a wild horse with a hornet in his ear till he has no more wind, and must needs pause to pump his lungs full again; a repetition of this indecency several times in a sermon is not uncommon, but is most painful. Pause soon enough to prevent that 'hough hough', which rather creates pity for the breathless orator than sympathy with the subject in hand. Your audience ought not to know that you breathe at all—the process of respiration should be as unobserved as the circulation of the blood. It is indecent to let the mere animal function of breathing cause any hiatus in your discourse.

Do not as a rule exert your voice to the utmost in ordinary preaching. Two or three earnest men, now present, are tearing themselves to pieces by needless bawling; their poor lungs are irritated, and their larynx inflamed by boisterous shouting, from which they seem unable to refrain. Now it is all very well to 'Cry aloud and spare not', but 'Do thyself no harm' is apostolical advice. When persons can hear you with half the amount of voice, it is as well to save the superfluous force for times when it may be wanted. 'Waste not, want not' may apply here as well as elsewhere. Be a little economical with that enormous volume of sound. Do not give your hearers head-aches when you mean to give them heart-aches: you aim to keep them from sleeping in their pews, but remember that it is not needful to burst the drums of their ears. 'The Lord is not in the wind.' Thunder is not lightning. Men do not hear in proportion to the noise created; in fact, too much noise stuns the ear, creates reverberations and echoes, and effectually injures the power of your sermons. Adapt your voice to your audience; when twenty thousand are before you, draw out the stops and give the full peal, but not in a room which will only hold a score or two. Whenever I enter a place to preach, I unconsciously calculate how much sound is needed to fill it, and after a few sentences my key is pitched. If you can make the man at the end of the chapel hear, if you can see that he is catching your thought, you may be sure that those nearer can hear you, and no more force is needed, perhaps a little less will do—watch and see. Why speak so as to be heard in the street when there is nobody there who is listening to you? Whether indoors or out, see that the most remote hearers can follow you, and that will be sufficient. By the way, I may observe, that brethren should out of mercy to the weak, always attend carefully to the force of their voices in sick rooms, and in congregations where some are known to be very infirm. It is a cruel thing to sit down by a sick man's bed-side, and shout out 'THE LORD IS MY SHEPHERD'. If you act so thoughtlessly, the poor man will say as soon as you are downstairs, 'Dear me! how my head aches. I am glad the good man is gone, Mary; that is a very precious Psalm and so quiet like, but he read it out like thunder and lightning, and almost stunned me!' Recollect, you younger and unmarried men, that soft whispers will suit the invalid better than roll of drum and culverin.

Observe carefully the rule to *vary the force of your voice*. The old rule was, to begin very softly, gradually rise higher, and bring out your loudest notes at the end. Let all such regulations be blown to pieces at the cannon's mouth; they are impertinent and misleading. Speak softly or loudly, as the emotion of the moment may suggest, and observe no artificial and fanciful rules. Artificial rules are an utter abomination. As M. de Cormorin satirically puts it, 'Be impassioned, thunder, rage, weep, up to the fifth word, of the third sentence, of the tenth paragraph, of the tenth leaf. How easy that would be! Above all, how very natural!' In imitation of a popular preacher, to whom it was unavoidable, a certain minister was accustomed in the commencement of his sermon to speak in so low a key, that no one could possibly hear him. Everybody leaned forward, fearing that something good was being lost in the air, but their straining was in vain, a holy mutter was all they could discern.

If the brother *could not* have spoken out none should have blamed him, but it was a most absurd thing to do this when in a short time he proved the power of his lungs by filling the whole structure by sonorous sentences. If the first half of his discourse was of no importance, why not omit it? and if of any value at all, why not deliver it distinctly? *Effect*, gentlemen, that was the point aimed at; he knew that one who spake in that fashion had produced great effects, and he hoped to rival him. If any of you dare commit such a folly for such a detestable object, I heartily wish you had never entered this Institution. I tell you most seriously, that the thing called '*effect*' is hateful, because it is untrue, artificial, tricky and therefore despicable. Never do anything for effect, but scorn the stratagems of little minds, hunting after the approval of connoisseurs in preaching, who are a race as obnoxious to a true minister as locusts to the Eastern husbandman. But I digress: be clear and distinct at the very first. Your exordia are too good to be whispered to space. Speak them out boldly, and command attention at the very outset by your manly tones. Do not start at the highest pitch as a rule, for then you will not be able to rise when you warm with the work; but still be outspoken from the first. Lower the voice when suitable even to a whisper; for soft, deliberate, solemn utterances are not only a relief to the ear, but have a great aptitude to reach the heart. Do not be afraid of the low keys, for if you throw force into them they are as well heard as the shouts. You need not speak in a loud voice in order to be heard well. Macaulay says of William Pitt, 'His voice, even when it sank to a whisper, was heard to the remotest benches of the House of Commons.' It has been well said that the most noisy gun is not the one which carries a ball the furthest: the crack of a rifle is anything but noisy. It is not the loudness of your voice, it is the force which you put into it that is effective. I am certain that I could whisper so as to be heard throughout every corner of our great Tabernacle, and I am equally certain that I could holloa and shout so that nobody could understand me. The thing could be done here, but perhaps the example is needless, as I fear some of you perform the business with remarkable success. Waves of air may dash upon the ear in such rapid succession that they create no translatable impression on the auditory nerve. Ink is necessary to write with, but if you upset the ink bottle over the sheet of paper, you convey no meaning thereby, so is it with sound; sound is the ink, but management is needed, not quantity, to produce an intelligible writing upon the ear. If your sole ambition be to compete with—

> Stentor the strong, endued with brazen lungs,
> Whose throat surpass'd the force of fifty tongues,

then bawl yourselves into Elysium as rapidly as possible, but if you wish to be understood, and so to be of service, shun the reproach of being 'impotent and loud'. You are aware that shrill sounds travel the farthest: the singular cry which is used by travellers in the wilds of Australia, owes its remarkable power to its shrillness. A bell will be heard much farther off than a drum; and, very singularly, the more musical a sound is the farther it travels. It is not the thumping of the piano which is needed, but the judicious sounding of the best keys. You will therefore feel at liberty to ease the strain very frequently in the direction of loudness, and you will be greatly relieving both the ears of the audience and your own lungs. Try all methods, from the sledge-hammer to the puff-ball. Be as gentle as a zephyr and as furious as a tornado. Be, indeed, just what every common-sense person is in his speech when he talks naturally, pleads vehemently, whispers confidentially, appeals plaintively, or publishes distinctly.

Next to the moderation of lung-force, I should place the rule, *modulate your tones*. Alter the key frequently and vary the strain constantly. Let the bass, the treble and the tenor, take their turn. I beseech you to do this out of pity to yourself and to those who hear you. God has mercy upon us and arranges all things to meet our cravings for variety; let us have mercy upon our fellow creatures, and not persecute them with the tedium of sameness. It is a most barbarous thing to inflict upon the tympanum of a poor fellow creature's ear the anguish of being bored and gimbleted with the same sound for half an hour. What swifter mode of rendering the mind idiotic or lunatic could be conceived than the perpetual droning of a beetle, or buzzing of a blue-bottle, in the organ of hearing? What dispensation have you by which you are to be tolerated in such cruelty to the helpless victims who sit under your drum-drum ministrations? Kind nature frequently spares the drone's unhappy victims the full effect of his tortures by steeping them in sweet repose. This, however, you do not desire; then speak with varied voice. How few ministers remember that monotony causes sleep. I fear the charge brought by a writer in the 'Imperial Review' is true to the letter of numbers of my brethren. 'We all know how the noise of running water, or the murmur of the sea, or the sighing of the south wind among the pines, or the moaning of wood-doves, induces a delicious dreamy languor. Far be it from us to say that the voice of a modern divine resembles, in the slightest degree, any of these sweet sounds, yet the effect is the same, and few can resist the drowsy influences of a lengthy dissertation, delivered without the slightest variation of tone or alteration of expression. Indeed, the very exceptional use of the phrase "an awakening discourse", even by those most familiar with such matters, conveys the implication that the great majority of pulpit harangues are of a decidedly soporific tendency. It is an ill case when the preacher

> Leaves his hearers perplex'd—
> Twixt the two to determine:
> "Watch and pray," says the text,
> "Go to sleep," says the sermon.'

However musical your voice may be in itself, if you continue to sound the same chord perpetually, your hearers will perceive that its notes are by distance made more sweet. Do in the name of humanity cease intoning and take to rational speaking. Should this argument fail to move you, I am so earnest about this point, that if you will not follow my advice out of mercy to your hearers, yet do it out of mercy to yourselves; for as God in his infinite wisdom has been pleased always to append a penalty to every sin against his natural as well as moral laws, so the evil of monotony is frequently avenged by that dangerous disease called *dysphonia clericorum*, or, 'Clergyman's sore throat'. When certain of our brethren are so beloved by their hearers that they do not object to pay a handsome sum to get rid of them for a few months, when a journey to Jerusalem is recommended and provided for, bronchitis of a modified order is so remarkably overruled for good, that my present argument will not disturb their equanimity; but such is not *our* lot, to us bronchitis means real misery, and therefore, to avoid it, we would follow any sensible suggestion. If you wish to ruin your throats you can speedily do so, but if you wish to preserve them, note what is now laid before you. I have often in this room compared the voice to a drum. If the drummer should always strike in one place on the head of his drum, the skin would soon wear into a hole; but how much longer it would have lasted him if he had varied his thumping and had used the entire surface of the drum-head! So it is with a man's voice. If he uses always the same tone, he will wear a hole in that part of the throat which is most exercised in producing that monotony, and very soon he will suffer from bronchitis. I have heard surgeons affirm, that Dissenting bronchitis differs from the Church of England article. There is an ecclesiastical twang which is much admired in the Establishment, a sort of steeple-in-the-throat grandeur, an aristocratic, theologic, parsonic, supernatural, infra-human mouthing of language and rolling over of words. It may be illustrated by the following specimen. 'He that hath yaws to yaw let him yaw,' which is a remarkable, if not impressive, rendering of a Scripture text. Who does not know the hallowed way of pronouncing 'Dearly beloved brethren, the Scripture moveth us in divers places'? It rolls in my ears now like Big Ben—coupled with boyish memories of monotonous peals of 'The Prince Albert, Albert Prince of Wales, and all the Royal Family … Amen'. Now, if a man who talks so unnaturally does *not* get bronchitis, or some other disease, I can only say that throat diseases must be very sovereignly dispensed. At the Nonconformist hobbies of utterance I have already struck a blow, and I believe it is by them that larynx and lungs become delicate, and good men succumb to silence and the grave. Should you desire my authority for the threat which I have held out to you, I shall give you the opinion of Mr Macready, the eminent tragedian, who, since he looks at the matter from an impartial but experimental standpoint, is worthy of a respectful hearing. 'Relaxed throat is usually caused, not so much by exercising the organ, as by the kind of exercise; that is, not so much by long or loud speaking, as by speaking in a feigned voice. I am not sure that I shall be understood in this statement, but there is not one person in, I may say, ten thousand, who in addressing a body of people, does so in his natural voice; and this habit is more especially observable in the pulpit. I believe that relaxation of the throat results from violent efforts in these affected tones, and that severe irritation, and often ulceration, is the consequence. The labour of a whole day's duty in a church is nothing, in point of labour, compared with the performance of one of Shakespeare's leading characters, nor I should suppose, with any of the very great displays made by our leading statesmen in the Houses of Parliament; and I feel very certain that the disorder, which you designate as "Clergyman's sore throat", is attributable generally to the mode of speaking, and not to the length of time or violence of effort that may be employed. I have known several of my former contemporaries on the stage suffer from sore throat, but I do not think, among those eminent in their art, that it could be regarded as a prevalent disease.' Actors and barristers have much occasion to strain their vocal powers, and yet there is no such thing as a counsel's sore throat, or a tragedian's bronchitis; simply because these men dare not serve the public in so slovenly a manner as some preachers serve their God. Samuel Fenwick, Esq., M.D., in a popular treatise upon 'Diseases of the Throat and Lungs' [A popular treatise on the 'Causes and Prevention of Diseases' by Samuel Fenwick, M.D., Volume I, 'Diseases of the Throat and Lungs' (John Churchill, New Burlington Street)] has most wisely said, 'From what was stated respecting the physiology of the vocal chords, it will be evident that continued speaking in one tone is much more fatiguing than frequent alterations in the pitch of the voice; because by the former, one muscle or set of muscles alone is strained, whilst by the latter, different muscles are brought into action, and thus relieve one another. In the same way, a man raising his arm at right angles to his body, becomes fatigued in five or ten minutes, because only one set of muscles has to bear the weight; but these same muscles can work the whole day if their action is alternated with that of others. Whenever, therefore, we hear a clergyman droning through the church service, and in the same manner and tone of voice reading, praying and exhorting, we may be perfectly sure that he is giving ten times more labour to his vocal chords than is absolutely necessary.'

This may be the place to reiterate an opinion which I have often expressed in this place, of which I am reminded by the author whom I have quoted. If ministers would speak oftener, their throats and lungs would be less liable to disease. Of this I am quite sure; it is matter of personal experience and wide observation, and I am confident that I am not mistaken. Gentlemen, twice-a-week preaching is very dangerous, but I have found five or six times healthy, and even twelve or fourteen not excessive. A costermonger set to cry cauliflowers and potatoes one day in the week, would find the effort most laborious, but when he for six successive days fills streets and lanes and alleys with his sonorous din, he finds no *dysphonia pomariorum*, or 'Costermonger's sore throat', laying him aside from his humble toils. I was pleased to find my opinion, that infrequent preaching is the root of many diseases, thus plainly declared by Dr Fenwick. 'All the directions which have been here laid down will, I believe, be ineffectual without regular daily practice of the voice. Nothing seems to have such a tendency to produce this disease as the occasional prolonged speaking, alternating with long intervals of rest, to which clergymen are more particularly subject. Anyone giving the subject a moment's consideration will readily understand this. If a man, or any other animal, be intended for any unusual muscular exertion, he is regularly exercised in it, day by day, and labour is thus rendered easy which otherwise it would be almost impossible to execute. But the generality of the clerical profession undergo a great amount of muscular exertion in the way of speaking only on one day of the week, whilst in the remaining six days they scarcely ever raise their voice above the usual pitch. Were a smith or a carpenter thus occasionally to undergo the fatigue connected with the exercise of his trade, he would not only be quite unfitted for it, but he would lose the skill he had acquired. The example of the most celebrated orators the world has seen proves the advantages of regular and constant practice of speaking; and I would on this account, most strongly recommend all persons subject to this complaint to read aloud once or twice a day, using the same pitch of voice as in the pulpit, and paying especial attention to the position of the chest and throat, and to clear and proper articulation of the words.' Mr Beecher is of the same opinion, for he remarks, 'Newsboys show what out-of-door practice will do for a man's lungs. What would the pale and feeble-speaking minister do who can scarcely make his voice reach two hundred auditors if he were set to cry newspapers? Those New York newsboys stand at the head of a street, and send down their voices through it, as an athletic would roll a ball down an alley. We advise men training for speaking professions to peddle wares in the streets for a little time. Young ministers might go into partnership with newsboys awhile, till they got their mouths open and their larynx nerved and toughened.'

Gentlemen, a needful rule is—*always suit your voice to your matter*. Do not be jubilant over a doleful subject, and on the other hand, do not drag heavily where the tones ought to trip along merrily, as though they were dancing to the tune of the angels in heaven. This rule I shall not enlarge upon, but rest assured it is of the utmost importance, and if obediently followed, will always secure attention, provided your matter is worth it. Suit your voice to your matter always, and, above all, *in everything be natural* [When Johnson was asked whether Burke resembled Tullius Cicero, 'No, Sir,' was the reply, 'he resembles Edmund Burke.'] Away for ever with slavish attention to rules and models. Do not imitate other people's voices, or, if from an unconquerable propensity you must follow them, emulate every orator's excellencies, and the evil will be lessened. I am myself, by a kind of irresistible influence, drawn to be an imitator, so that a journey to Scotland or Wales will for a week or two materially affect my pronunciation and tone. Strive against it I do, but there it is, and the only cure I know of is to let the mischief die a natural death. Gentlemen, I return to my rule— use your own natural voices. Do not be monkeys, but men; not parrots, but men of originality in all things. It is said that the most becoming way for a man to wear his beard is that in which it grows, for both in colour and form it will suit his face. Your own modes of speech will be most in harmony with your methods of thought and your own personality. The mimic is for the playhouse, the cultured man in his sanctified personality is for the sanctuary. I would repeat this rule till I wearied you if I thought you would forget it; be natural, be natural, be natural evermore. An affectation of voice, or an imitation of the manner of Dr Silvertongue, the eminent divine, or even of a well-beloved tutor or president will inevitably ruin you. I charge you to throw away the servility of imitation and rise to the manliness of originality.

We are bound to add—*endeavour to educate your voice.* Grudge no pains or labour in achieving this, for as it has been well observed, 'However prodigious may be the gifts of nature to her elect, they can only be developed and brought to their extreme perfection by labour and study.' Think of Michael Angelo working for a week without taking off his clothes, and Handel hollowing out every key of his harpsichord, like a spoon, by incessant practice. Gentlemen, after this, never talk of difficulty or weariness. It is almost impossible to see the utility of Demosthenes' method of speaking with stones in his mouth, but any one can perceive the usefulness of his pleading with the boisterous billows, that he might know how to command a hearing amidst the uproarious assemblies of his countrymen; and in his speaking as he ran up-hill that his lungs might gather force from laborious use the reason is as obvious as the self-denial is commendable. We are bound to use every possible means to perfect the voice by which we are to tell forth the glorious gospel of the blessed God. Take great care of the consonants, enunciate every one of them clearly; they are the features and expression of the words. Practise indefatigably till you give every one of the consonants its due; the vowels have a voice of their own, and therefore they can speak for themselves. In all other matters exercise a rigid discipline until you have mastered your voice, and have it in hand like a well-trained steed. Gentlemen with narrow chests are advised to use the dumb-bells every morning, or better still, those clubs which the College has provided for you. You need broad chests, and must do your best to get them. Do not speak with your hands in your waistcoat pockets so as to contract your lungs, but throw the shoulders back as public singers do. Do not lean over a desk while speaking, and never hold the head down on the breast while preaching. Upward rather than downward let the body bend. Off with all tight cravats and button-up waistcoats; leave room for the full play of the bellows and the pipes. Observe the statues of the Roman or Greek orators, look at Raphael's picture of Paul, and, without affectation, fall naturally into the graceful and appropriate attitudes there depicted, for these are best for the voice. Get a friend to tell you your faults, or better still, welcome an enemy who will watch you keenly and sting you savagely. What a blessing such an irritating critic will be to a wise man, what an intolerable nuisance to a fool! Correct yourself diligently and frequently, or you will fall into errors unawares, false tones will grow, and slovenly habits will form insensibly; therefore criticize yourself with unceasing care. Think nothing little by which you may be even a little more useful. But, gentlemen, never degenerate in this business into pulpit fops, who think gesture and voice to be everything. I am sick at heart when I hear of men taking a whole week to get up a sermon, much of the getting up consisting in repeating their precious productions before a glass! Alas! for this age, if graceless hearts are to be forgiven for the sake of graceful manners. Give us all the vulgarities of the wildest back-woods' itinerant rather than the perfumed prettinesses of effeminate gentility. I would no more advise you to be fastidious with your voices than I would recommend you to imitate Rowland Hill's Mr Taplash with his diamond ring, his richly scented pocket handkerchief and his eyeglass. Exquisites are out of place in the pulpit, they should be set up in a tailor's window, with a ticket, 'This style complete, including MSS, £10 10s.'

Perhaps here may be the place to observe, that it were well if all parents were more attentive to the teeth of their children, since faulty teeth may cause serious damage to a speaker. There are men, whose articulation is faulty, who should at once consult the dentist— I mean, of course, a thoroughly scientific and experienced one; for a few false teeth or some other simple arrangement would be a permanent blessing to them. My own dentist very sensibly remarks in his circular, 'When a portion or the whole of the teeth are lost, a contraction of the muscles of the face and throat follows, the other organs of the voice which have been accustomed to the teeth are impaired, and put out of their common play, producing a break, languor or depression, as in a musical instrument which is deficient in a note. It is vain to expect perfect symphony, and proportional and consistent accent on the key, tone and pitch of the voice, with deficiencies in its organs, and of course the articulation becomes defective; such defect adds much to the *labour* of speaking, to say the least, and in most cases lisping, a too hasty or sudden drop, or a faint delivery, is the result; from more serious deficiencies a mumbling and clattering is almost sure to follow.' Where this is the mischief, and the cure is within reach, we are bound for our work's sake to avail ourselves of it. Teeth may seem unimportant, but be it remembered, that nothing is little in so great a calling as ours. I shall in succeeding remarks mention even smaller matters, but it is with the deep impression that hints upon insignificant things may be of unknown value in saving you from serious neglects or gross errors.

Lastly, I would say with regard to your throats—*take care of them*. Take care always to clear them well when you are about to speak, but do not be constantly clearing them while you are preaching. A very esteemed brother of my acquaintance always talks in this way—'My dear friends—hem—hem—this is a most—hem—important subject which I have now—hem—hem—to bring before you, and—hem—hem—I have to call upon you to give me—hem—hem—your most serious—hem—attention.' [A young preacher, desirous of improving his style, wrote to Jacob Gruber for advice. He had contracted the habit of prolonging his words, especially when under excitement. The old gentleman sent him the following laconic reply. 'Dear—ah! brother—ah!—When—ah you—ah go—ah to—ah preach—ah, take — ah care — ah you—ah do not—ah say—ah ah—ah!—Yours—ah, Jacob—ah Gruber—ah.'] Avoid this most zealously. Others, from want of clearing the throat, talk as if they were choked up, and were just about to expectorate; it were far better to do so at once than to sicken the hearer by repeated unpleasant sounds. Snuffling and sniffing are excusable enough when a man has a cold, but they are extremely unpleasant, and when they become habitual, they ought to be indicted under the 'Nuisances Act'. Pray excuse me, it may appear vulgar to mention such things, but your attention to the plain and free observations made in this lecture room may save many remarks at your expense hereafter.

When you have done preaching take care of your throat by *never wrapping it up tightly*. From personal experience I venture with some diffidence to give this piece of advice. If any of you possess delightfully warm woollen comforters, with which there may be associated the most tender remembrances of mother or sister, treasure them—treasure them in the bottom of your trunk, but do not expose them to any vulgar use by wrapping them round your necks. If any brother wants to die of influenza let him wear a warm scarf round his neck, and then one of these nights he will forget it, and catch such a cold as will last him the rest of his natural life. You seldom see a sailor wrap his neck up. No, he always keeps it bare and exposed, and has a turn-down collar, and if he has a tie at all, it is but a small one loosely tied, so that the wind can blow all round his neck. In this philosophy I am a firm believer, having never deviated from it for these fourteen years, and having before that time been frequently troubled with colds, but very seldom since. If you feel that you want something else, why, then grow your beards! A habit most natural, scriptural, manly and beneficial.

One of our brethren, now present, has for years found this of great service. He was compelled to leave England on account of the loss of his voice, but he has become as strong as Samson now that his locks are unshorn. If your throats become affected consult a good physician, or if you cannot do this, give what attention you please to the following hint. Never purchase 'Marsh-mallow Rock', 'Cough-no-more Lozenges', 'Pulmonic Wafers', Horehound, Ipecacuanha or any of the ten thousand emollient compounds. They may serve your turn for a time by removing present uneasiness, but they ruin the throat by their laxative qualities. If you wish to improve your throat take a good share of pepper—good Cayenne pepper, and other astringent substances, as much as your stomach can bear; do not go beyond that, because you must recollect that you have to take care of your stomach as well as your throat, and if the digesting apparatus be out of order, nothing can be right. Common sense teaches you that astringents must be useful. Did you ever hear of a tanner making a piece of hide into leather by laying it to soak in sugar? Neither would tolu, ipecacuanha or treacle serve his purpose, but the very reverse; if he wants to harden and strengthen the skin, he places it in a solution of oak-bark, or some astringent substance which draws the material together and strengthens it. When I began to preach at Exeter Hall my voice was weak for such a place—as weak as the usual run of voices, and it had frequently failed me altogether in street preaching, but in Exeter Hall (which is an unusually difficult place to preach in, from its excessive width in proportion to its length), I always had a little glass of Chilli vinegar and water just in front of me, a draught of which appeared to give a fresh force to the throat, whenever it grew weary and the voice appeared likely to break down. When my throat becomes a little relaxed I usually ask the cook to prepare me a basin of beef-tea, as strong with pepper as can be borne, and hitherto this has been a sovereign remedy. However, as I am not qualified to practise in medicine, you will probably pay no more attention to me in medical matters than to any other quack. My belief is that half the difficulties connected with the voice in our early days will vanish as we advance in years, and find in use a second nature. I would encourage the truly earnest to persevere; if they feel the Word of the Lord like fire in their bones, even stammering may be overcome, and fear, with all its paralysing results, may be banished. Take heart, young brother, persevere, and God, and nature, and practice, will help you.

I shall not detain you longer, but express the hope that your chest, lungs, windpipe, larynx and all your vocal organs may last you till you have nothing more to say.

FOR FURTHER HELP AND INFORMATION

Books

Patsy Rodenburg, *The Right to Speak: Working with the Voice* (London: Methuen, 1995)

Barbara Houseman, *Finding Your Voice: A Step-by Step Guide for Actors* (London: Nick Hern Books, 2002)

Cicely Berry, OBE, *Your Voice and How to Use It* (London: Virgin Books, 1994)

The Voice Care Network publishes the following:

> *More Care For Your Voice*
> *Voice Warm-up Exercises* (A6 booklet)
> *Keeping a Young Voice*

Websites

The Voice Care Network
25 The Square, Kenilworth
CV8 1EF
Tel./Fax 01926 864000
www.voicecare.org.uk
info@voicecare.org.uk

The British Voice Association
The Institute of Laryngology & Otology
330 Gray's Inn Road
London, WC1X 8EE
Tel. 020 7713 0064
www.british-voice-association.com
bva@diran.co.uk

(Both the VCN and the BFA have good, free information on voice care on their websites.)

ENDNOTES

1 James L. Snyder, *In Pursuit of God: The Life of A. W. Tozer* (Camp Hill, PA: Christian Publications, 1991), pp. 108–109.

2 George Newton, quoted by Iain Murray in 'Biographical Introduction', Joseph Alleine, *Alarm to the Unconverted* (London: Banner of Truth, 1967), p. 9.

3 C. H. Spurgeon, 'On the Voice', Lecture viii, *Lectures to My Students* (Grand Rapids, MI: Baker, 1980), p. 121. (See Appendix 3 for complete lecture.)

4 Richard Bewes, *Speaking in Public Effectively* (Fearn: Christian Focus, 2002), p. 96.

5 Dr P. Masters, *Physicians of Souls* (London: Wakeman, 2002), p. 172.

6 Spurgeon, 'On the Voice', p.122

7 Ibid., p. 121.

8 Ibid., p. 131.

9 Ibid., p. 125.

10 Ingvar Haddal, *John Wesley: A Biography* (London: Epworth Press, 1961), pp. 112–113.

11 Revd John Wesley, 'Preface', *Primitive Physick* (London: W. Strahan, 1761), p. xi.

12 William R. Moody, *The Life of Dwight L. Moody* (London: Morgan & Scott, [1900?]), pp. 397–398.

13 Brief history obtained from Oswald Penry, an elder at Litchard Mission Church, Bridgend, South Wales.

14 Handley C. G. Moule, *Charles Simeon* (London: InterVarsity Press, 1948), p. 127.

ABOUT DAY ONE:

Day One's threefold commitment:

- To be faithful to the Bible, God's inerrant, infallible Word;
- To be relevant to our modern generation;
- To be excellent in our publication standards.

I continue to be thankful for the publications of Day One. They are biblical; they have sound theology; and they are relevant to the issues at hand. The material is condensed and manageable while, at the same time, being complete—a challenging balance to find. We are happy in our ministry to make use of these excellent publications.

JOHN MACARTHUR, PASTOR-TEACHER, GRACE COMMUNITY CHURCH, CALIFORNIA

It is a great encouragement to see Day One making such excellent progress. Their publications are always biblical, accessible and attractively produced, with no compromise on quality. Long may their progress continue and increase!

JOHN BLANCHARD, AUTHOR, EVANGELIST AND APOLOGIST

Visit our web site for more information and
to request a free catalogue of our books.

www.dayone.co.uk

Coming Soon

Discipline with care
Applying biblical correction in your church

STEPHEN MCQUOID

ISBN 978-1-84625-152-8

Discipline is one of the most difficult issues in contemporary church life. Church leaders often need to battle to maintain the integrity of their churches, sometimes with tragic results. But why is it so hard? Should we bother with it at all?

In this thorough treatment of the subject, Stephen McQuoid answers these questions and provides a biblical framework for church discipline. Because prevention is better than cure, he shows that discipline is not just about punishing but includes a whole way of life which keeps us spiritually accountable and in a right relationship with God. Corrective discipline will also at times be necessary, and he guides us through the disciplinary stages taught in the New Testament. By using appropriate case studies, he also demonstrates the complications of real-life situations and highlights the lessons that can be learned.

'Stephen McQuoid emphasises the need for leaders not to shirk the correction of members no matter how difficult. In exercising discipline the church is giving God's verdict on the given situation. There must, therefore, be both judgement and compassion. Helpful advice is given to both leaders and members as to what kind of attitude should be displayed towards the offender.'

DAVID CLARKSON, ELDER AT CARTSBRIDGE EVANGELICAL CHURCH AND AUTHOR OF 'LEARNING TO LEAD' COURSE

'In any local church, the issues of authority, discipline and leadership lie close to the surface. Stephen's book explores succinctly some of the cultural issues, scriptural context and practical outworkings of the vital need to keep the body in shape.'

ANDREW LACEY, CHURCH ELDER, MANAGER GLO BOOK SHOP, DIRECTOR OF PARTNERSHIP, SCOTLAND

Coming Soon

Make your church's money work
Achieving financial integrity in your congregation

JOHN TEMPLE

ISBN 978-1-84625-150-4

The church's finances are a real concrete expression of its vision, its priorities and its commitment to doing things 'decently and in order'. This book examines the basis of sound biblical stewardship as applied to the practical aspects of budgeting, reporting and control of expenses in a church. It suggests a remuneration policy for pastors and other paid workers and outlines the responsibilities of members in supporting their church. Examples of a spreadsheet for budgeting and reporting are included in Appendix B. It is written in non accounting terminology and should be read by all leaders and anyone who spends any of the church's money.

Coming Soon

Visit the Sick
Shepherding the afflicted and dying in your congregation

BRIAN CROFT

ISBN 978-1-84625-143-6

The demands of the twenty-first-century have led to the neglect of certain essential responsibilities in the life of a Christian. One of those is the visitation and care of the sick in our congregations. This book is designed to instruct and motivate pastors, church leaders, and other care-giving Christians through the counsel of our heroes of church history, to recapture the practice of visiting the sick. This is accomplished by considering three specific areas. First, is our commitment to the theological as we consider how to most effectively care for their souls. Second, is our commitment to the pastoral, which instructs us how to proceed with wisdom and discernment in the variety of circumstances we will face. Third, is our commitment to the practical so that the manner in which we care for the sick will help, not hinder our effort to communicate biblical truth to them.

'Many younger pastors (and not so young ones as well) have never received the sort of very practical guidance which Brian Croft gives in this book. It will now be a recommended text in my Pastoral Ministries class.'

RAY VAN NESTE, PH.D., ASSOCIATE PROFESSOR OF CHRISTIAN STUDIES, DIRECTOR, R. C. RYAN CENTER FOR BIBLICAL STUDIES, UNION UNIVERSITY, ELDER, CORNERSTONE COMMUNITY CHURCH

'Church member, let this book equip you to become more useful to those in your church who are ailing. Young pastor, gain from Brian's practical wisdom. Seasoned pastor, let this book remind you of the privilege it is to serve and encourage the sick in a fallen world. I plan to read it together with our elders, and hope to make it available to our congregation as an equipping tool.'

PAUL ALEXANDER, SENIOR PASTOR, FOX VALLEY BIBLE CHURCH, ST. CHARLES, IL, CO-AUTHOR, THE DELIBERATE CHURCH